W9-CGY-475

IMAGES
of Motoring

FORD DYNASTY

A PHOTOGRAPHIC HISTORY

On July 30, 1963, to celebrate the 100th Anniversary of Henry Ford's birth, the Henry Ford Trade School Alumni Association commissioned this bust of the industrialist. It was displayed in the lobby of Ford Motor Company's World Headquarters building in Dearborn, Michigan, just a mile southwest of the original location of his farmstead birthplace. The Trade School was one of numerous sidelines in the still-controversial life of the man "who put the world on wheels" while establishing a dynastic industrial empire. (N)

IMAGES
of Motoring

FORD DYNASTY

A PHOTOGRAPHIC HISTORY

Michael W.R. Davis and
James K. Wagner

ARCADIA

Copyright © 2002 by Michael W.R. Davis and James K. Wagner
ISBN 978-0-7385-2039-1

Published by Arcadia Publishing
Charleston SC, Chicago IL, Portsmouth NH, San Francisco CA

Printed in the United States of America

Library of Congress Catalog Card Number: 2002111105

For all general information contact Arcadia Publishing at:
Telephone 843-853-2070
Fax 843-853-0044
E-mail sales@arcadiapublishing.com
For customer service and orders:
Toll-Free 1-888-313-2665

Visit us on the Internet at www.arcadiapublishing.com

At the New York Auto Show display of its 1941 models, Edsel Ford (center), the only child of Henry Ford and president of Ford Motor Company at the time, stood with his oldest sons Henry Ford II (left) and Benson Ford. Henry II and Benson were soon to become the third generation of their family involved in active management of the auto company. As indicated by signs in the background, Ford Motor Company's car models then included Deluxe and Super Deluxe Ford, Mercury, Lincoln Zephyr, Lincoln Custom, and Lincoln Continental. (N)

CONTENTS

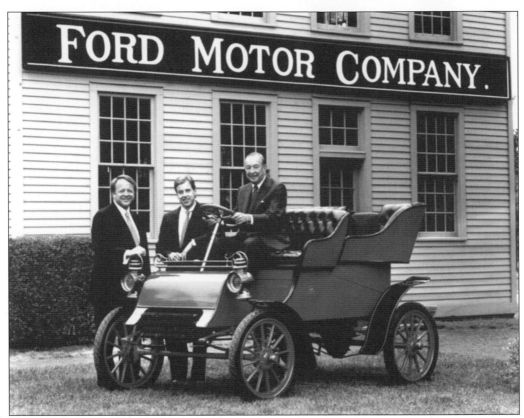

To mark the 90th anniversary of Ford Motor Company's founding, third- and fourth-generation Ford family members posed in Greenfield Village at a replica of the company's first factory with a restored 1903 Ford Model A, the company's first production car. From left are Edsel Ford II, a Ford Company vice president serving at the time as president of Ford Motor Credit Company, and son of Henry Ford II; William Clay Ford Jr., destined to become chairman of the board; and his father, William Clay Ford, vice chairman of the company, one-time general manager of Continental Division and youngest son of Edsel Ford. By the year 2001, a fifth-generation family member, Elena Ford, granddaughter of Henry Ford II, had become an active member of Ford management. (N)

ACKNOWLEDGMENTS

The authors wish to acknowledge the infinite patience of their wives, Karen Davis and Ann Wagner, in the many months they were cast into the roles of "computer widows" during the production of this book. We especially want to thank Mark Patrick, Barbara Thompson, and Laura Kotsis of the National Automotive History Collection at the Detroit Public Library; Tom Featherstone of the Walter P. Reuther Library at Wayne State University, and Mike Skinner of the Henry Ford Heritage Association for assistance with historical images. And we are indebted to Karen Davis moreover for her diligent and expert copyediting.

INTRODUCTION

Books about Ford Motor Company and the Ford family are truly a cottage industry: there are more than 200 in print, not counting dozens of car books devoted to specialized Ford subjects like V-8s and Mustangs.

After Henry Ford drew international attention in 1914 with this announcement of the Five Dollar Day, he became a folk hero. The press quoted him at length from every utterance. To this day, the Ford family has probably received more media attention, certainly in the U.S., than even the royal family of Britain.

So it is hard for Ford historians to find something new to say. And for a picture history book like this, it was hard to find many images that haven't been published countless times. Indeed, to move the narrative of *Ford Dynasty* along, some familiar images had to be used. There are, however, a number of original images that have never before been published.

It is entirely appropriate that *Ford Dynasty* is published on the eve of Ford Motor Company's centennial of its June 1903 founding, although this—and indeed, many a Ford history—begins with the founder's birth 40 years earlier.

Notably this book is a special labor of love. As noted on the back cover, the co-authors spent a total of 63 years working for Ford Motor Company, bringing a unique perspective to its history. What you see and read here is their shared long view of the company.

Mike Davis and Jim Wagner enjoyed their childhoods with a Ford as the family car. Their tales follow.

The first Davis car, long before Mike's birth, was a second-hand Model T. Mike's earliest car memory is the family's dark blue 1935 Fordor (Ford's unique way of describing a four-door sedan) with distinctive red wire wheels. Before that first memory, there had been a family '32 Ford V-8 sedan with an interesting story. Mike's dad was a part-time daily newspaper columnist who was given the car by the newspaper as payment for a year's worth of columns; the newspaper, in turn, had received the car from a local Ford dealer in exchange for advertising. No money had changed hands: that's the way things were in 1932, arguably the worst year of the Depression.

The Davis family photo album shows '37 and '39 Deluxe Fordors, which Mike remembers as dark green. He recalls the wonder of the '37's new "alligator" hood, opened by twisting the hood ornament.

Years later, as a newspaper reporter in Miami, the first auto company executives and public relations people Mike met were from Ford. When offered a choice of news bureau jobs with *Business Week*, he selected Detroit because he had always been a "car nut." And when *Business Week* wanted to promote him to New York, he decided to stay in Detroit. Ford Motor was the first place he looked for a local job, and he spent the next 25 years on the public relations staff.

Mike retired from Ford in 1985 as marketing projects manager for North American Automotive Operations, after stints in a variety of staff and divisional positions.

Jim recalls a high school discussion about cars when a classmate remarked, "Wagner, you cut your teeth on a Ford steering wheel!" He was indeed born into a "Ford family." Both of his father's older brothers were involved with Model Ts and Fordson tractors, one of them managing a long-operating Ford Neighborhood Service Station. Their beloved local dealer, Fred Potschner, who represented Ford for nearly 58 years, nurtured this loyalty. Thus Jim's first knowing encounter with an automobile was the family 1936 Ford V-8 Tudor Trunk Sedan, and his first new car was a '61 purchased from Potschner.

Like Mike, Jim doesn't recall how he became a "car nut." He remembers being intrigued by the bright blue oval and chrome "V-8" hood ornament on the front of the family car as well as car, truck, and farm tractor advertisements in prewar magazines, and the issues of *Ford News* that abounded in his grandmother's rural home. When the first postwar Ford arrived at the local dealer in 1945, Jim recalls going to see it, as well as eagerly anticipating arrival of the all-new '49 Ford, Mercury, and Lincoln. During this time he began his life-long hobby of collecting automotive literature.

In due course he became a mechanical engineer and joined Ford Motor Company as an engineer in 1963. After a decade in passenger car development, he moved to Truck Engineering and later to a position as a project manager at the Automotive Safety Office, from which he retired in 2000.

The partnership of these two car nuts to produce *Ford Dynasty* was a natural.

Following is the key to photo credits found in parentheses at the end of each caption:

D	Michael W. R. Davis, personal collection
F	Ford Motor Company Communications
G	The Archives at Henry Ford Museum and Greenfield Village
H	The Archives at Henry Ford Hospital
I	Indianapolis Motor Speedway Museum
N	National Automotive History Collection, Detroit Public Library
P	Ford Motor Company Photomedia Archives
R	Walter P. Reuther Library, Wayne State University
S	Michael Skinner, personal collection
W	James K. Wagner, personal collection

One

HENRY FORD AND THE INFANT AUTO INDUSTRY

1863–1902

This photograph of a moustachioed Henry Ford in his first experimental car, the Quadricycle, was taken in October 1896 as a re-enactment of his first journey in the gas buggy on the streets of Detroit that had occurred some four months earlier on the morning of June 4. He was 33 and held a good job as chief engineer of Edison Illuminating Company. Henry had already travelled far from his family's farm to meet his idol, Thomas A. Edison, at an electric industry meeting in New York. His choice to run a motor car might have more logically been a steam engine, familiar from farm days, or electric batteries from his work at Edison. He had however been working on the bicycle- and buggy-based Quadricycle and its gasoline engine for about three years, studying reports in magazines such as *American Machinist, Popular Science,* and *Scientific American,* and exchanging views with other neighborhood tinkerers. And he still would face a series of setbacks before advent of the lasting Ford Motor Company seven years later. (F)

Henry Ford's birthplace, pictured here before its restoration, was a typical Greek Revival Michigan farmhouse of the mid-19th century. It was built by his father William Ford in about 1860 with timber from woods on his 40-acre farm. (D)

The Ford farmstead, as shown in an 1876 Wayne County Atlas, stood on Greenfield Road at the southeast corner of what is now Ford Road in Dearborn, west of Detroit. The farms of numerous Anglo-Irish relatives were nearby. In 1944, the seven-room birthplace was moved about two miles to Greenfield Village, the historical park and tourist attraction. (S)

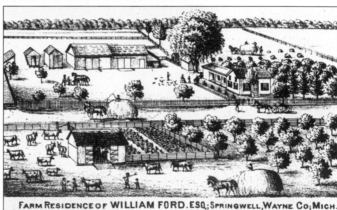

FARM RESIDENCE OF WILLIAM FORD. ESQ.; SPRINGWELL, WAYNE CO; MICH.

These two images show Henry Ford as a child of about 3 (above) and as a young man of 18 when he was an apprentice at a Detroit marine engine works. (D)

After various mechanical apprenticeships, Henry Ford found gainful employment repairing and operating steam farm engines and sawing lumber back in the rural area west of Detroit. In 1888, he married Clara Bryant and a year later built this "square" or "honeymoon" house for her at Southfield and Ford Roads, a mile west of his birthplace. (R)

Henry and Clara returned to Detroit in 1891 where he took a $40 a month position as an engineer with Edison Illuminating Co., one of three electric lighting companies in the city. He is shown here (top row, third from right) with the Edison station-house crew. He stayed at Edison for eight years, during which time he bought his first bicycle and his first camera and, in off-hours, experimented with internal-combustion engines. (S)

At left is the duplex at 58 Bagley—three short blocks from Henry's job at Edison—which the Fords rented from 1893 to 1897. (P)

Pictured above are Henry Ford and his four-year-old son, Edsel, in 1898. (D)

Pictured is the famous woodshed/workshop behind 58 Bagley where Henry struggled for three years to perfect his first operable car, the Quadricycle. According to legend, he used an axe to bust out bricks around the right-hand door (photographed in 1897, probably by Henry himself) so he could roll the vehicle out for its first run early on the morning of June 4, 1896. (N)

This is Henry Ford on his Quadricycle in fall 1896. This first simple vehicle had no reverse or brakes, but Henry had mastered fundamentals such as crude carburetion that allowed it to run reliably. He sold it for about $200 late in 1896 to another young man experimenting locally with cars, Charles Annesley. (N) At right is a close-up of the engine. (W)

From 1897 to mid-1899, Henry continued at Edison Illuminating and used his personal time trying to improve on his gasoline motor car which, like other primitive gas buggies of the time, took on more of the appearance of a carriage. This is his so-called "second car" of 1897–1898. It still utilized modified bicycle wheels despite a weight gain of 375 pounds from the 500-pound Quadricycle. (N)

13

In August 1899, Henry quit Edison to join the Detroit Automobile Co., which was financed by an investor group of prominent citizens and businessmen. The venture failed and investors bailed out in early 1901 after losing $86,000. Henry then decided to demonstrate his automotive expertise by winning races. Here, he and his fourth car (#4) overtake a Winton in October 1901. (N)

After winning the Winton race, Henry attracted a new batch of investors who formed the Henry Ford Company late in 1901. Henry broke with them after only four months and made this new racer, 999—significantly, a front-engine design—which roared to success late in 1902. The company he had left behind changed its name and became Cadillac. (N)

Two

FORD MOTOR COMPANY AND THE MODELS THAT PUT THE WORLD ON WHEELS

1903–1910

This stock certificate was issued to Henry Ford on June 26, 1903, ten days after Ford Motor Company was organized. The number of shares totaled 255. They were par-valued at $100 each—his portion of a $150,000 initial capitalization, $100,000 of which was in cash with the remainder treasury stock. Mr. Ford's title was vice president while John S. Gray, a banker, was president of the firm bearing Ford's name. Other stockholders included Alexander Malcomson, John F. and Horace E. Dodge, Albert Strelow, Vernon C. Fry, C.H. Bennett, Horace H. Rackham, John W. Anderson, Charles J. Woodall, and James Couzens. Gray, Ford, Malcomson, John F. Dodge, and Anderson were directors. Malcomson was treasurer, and Couzens was secretary of the new company. Unofficially, Ford was in charge of production and Couzens headed business affairs. (D)

Ford Motor Company's first production facility was this rented building at 688–692 Mack Avenue in Detroit. Initially Ford cars were assembled from components made by other firms rather than from parts manufactured by the Company. Dodge Brothers supplied complete chassis, including engines, while C.R. Wilson Carriage Company provided bodies. Since Wilson also made bodies for Cadillac Automobile Company, the first Ford and the first Cadillac appeared quite similar. (S)

Heavy demand for the original Ford Model A, whose production totaled 1,708 during its first year, resulted almost immediately in adding a second floor to the factory. Even with twice the space, the Mack Avenue plant would soon be inadequate. (R)

This unrestored Ford Model A was displayed at the Automotive Industry Golden Jubilee celebration in 1946. Features of the $950 vehicle included an underseat-mounted two-cylinder engine. Though typically considered a 1903 model, Model A production continued well into a second year. (R)

Introduced in 1904, the Model B was Ford's first four-cylinder car and also its first with a front-mounted vertical engine and side-entrance body. Billed as one of "The Big Four of the Ford Line" for 1905, its $2,000 price made it the most expensive Ford thus far. "Four" meant four models, not cylinders. (N)

This evidently restored 1905 Model C was another pioneer Ford displayed at the Automotive Industry Golden Jubilee. Direct successor to the original Model A and one of the "Big Four," it sold for $850 as a two-place runabout and was promoted to physicians as "The Doctor's Car." (R)

Still another of the "Big Four" was the 1905 Model F, a more sophisticated version of the two-cylinder Model C. Compared with the Model C, the F was more powerful and had larger wheels and a longer wheelbase. It was also more expensive with a list price of $1,200. (N)

The inadequacy of the Ford Mack Avenue plant was clearly evident by 1904. In April of that year, company directors authorized the purchase of land for a new facility at Piquette Avenue and Beaubien Street in Detroit. Occupation began in December of that year and continued into 1905. The new Piquette Avenue plant would only serve the company until 1910. (R)

As the oldest extant one-time Ford property outside Greenfield Village, the Piquette plant is currently the object of an extensive restoration effort under the auspices of the Henry Ford Heritage Foundation. There is an ongoing campaign to have it placed in the National Register of Historic Places. This photo was taken in the late 1990s. (D)

Here Henry Ford is pictured driving a 1906 Ford Model K with company official LeRoy Pelletier at his left. Mrs. Pelletier is behind her husband, accompanying Clara and Edsel Ford. Championed by treasurer Alexander Malcomson, the six-cylinder $2,800 Model K was quite controversial within the company since it was intended for the typical well-to-do buyer and contrary to Henry Ford's vision of a "car for the multitudes." (N)

The Ford Model N contrasted sharply with its Model K contemporary and was more in accord with Henry Ford's philosophy. It was a significant improvement over the earlier Models A and C and, at $600, a far better value. Unlike its predecessors, the Model N featured a four-cylinder front-mounted engine while continuing the two-speed planetary transmission. Company sales exceeded 8,400 units for the 1906–1907 fiscal year—clear testimony to its success. (N)

The absence of Model Ks in this November 1, 1906 picture clearly indicates that production of the new Model R dominated contemporary activities at the company's Piquette Avenue plant. At this stage these chassis were not only missing bodies and fenders, but also driveshafts, rear axles, and springs. (P)

This c. 1998 picture of the Piquette Avenue plant shows the empty interior of the space, virtually unchanged after nearly a century. The 1904 vintage structure reflects wooden-beamed industrial architecture typical of the 1890s rather than the new school of reinforced concrete design soon to be seen in the work of Detroit architect Albert Kahn. Following his pioneering construction of the Packard plant, Kahn would build Ford facilities around the world. (D)

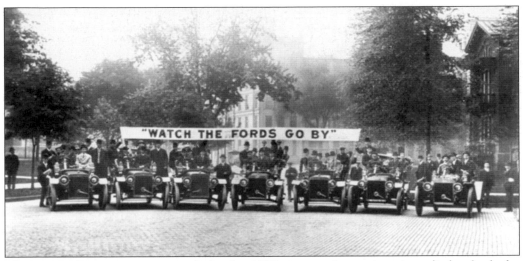

"Controversy" is an appropriate title for this 1907 vintage picture since it applied to both the depicted Ford Model Ks and the origin of the slogan emblazoned on the banner. "Watch The Fords Go By" was reportedly coined by W.S. Hogue, factory traffic manager, but the claim was challenged by Mrs. LeRoy Pelletier who insisted that her husband was its creator. Ford used the slogan repeatedly over the years. (N)

Henry Ford is actually among those seated at the table here, although he cannot be seen. The banquet was a sales promotional event with the theme "Make '07 a Ford Year." Given the concurrent economic panic, business proved less than ideal for Ford Motor Company. Sales for fiscal 1907–1908 dropped by more than 2,000 units (roughly 25 percent) compared with the previous sales season. (P)

Introduced for the 1907 season, Ford's Model R was a deluxe edition of the Model N, which remained in production. The R was list priced at $750, came only as a Runabout, and included such features as a 15-horsepower four-cylinder engine, running boards, 84-inch wheelbase, 30-inch (vs. 28-inch) tires and standard lamps and horn. Production continued into 1909, despite arrival of the Model T. (N)

Henry Ford was ever mindful of his rural background and, as attested by his experiments with agricultural machines, devoted considerable effort to improving the farmer's lot. This 1908 vintage picture shows the "automobile plow" which he built the previous year. Its four-cylinder engine and transmission came from a Ford Model B, while radiator, steering gear, and hubs were of Model K origin. (N)

The venue: New York Auto Show of 1908 when Ford was selling Models R (center), S, and K (right). Specific catalogued body styles were Model R and Model S Runabouts, Model K and Model S Roadsters, and the 40-horsepower Model K Touring Car. Model S was similar to Model R except that it included a single rear seat, sometimes called a "mother-in-law seat." (N)

The Ford Model T has been called "The car that put America on wheels." When introduced on October 1, 1908, it was considered technically advanced, incorporating such features as a flywheel magneto, planetary transmission, and transverse-leaf front and rear springs. Selling for $850, the Model T Touring Car was such an outstanding value that company sales increased to 10,607 for the ensuing fiscal year. (W)

Henry Ford moved his family into this spacious brick home on Detroit's prestigious Edison Avenue in 1908. During the first 20 years of their marriage, the Fords moved frequently. This house would be the Fords' final Detroit home before building their Fair Lane mansion along the Rouge River in Dearborn. Jerry Mitchell, the man heading preservation of the Piquette Avenue plant, lives in the Edison house today. (N)

Henry Ford is shown here around 1909 in his Piquette plant office. He had succeeded John S. Gray as president of the company in 1906, reached his goal of the "universal car" with the Model T in 1908, and had passed up an overture to join General Motors early in 1909. In another couple of years, he would best the Selden suit and be a millionaire several times over. (S)

Three

MIRACLE OF MASS PRODUCTION AND WORLD WAR I

1911–1920

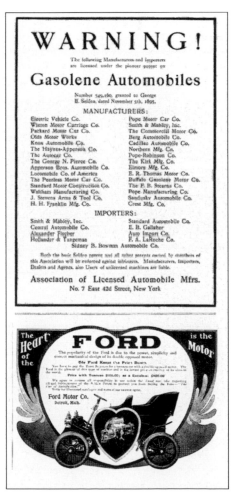

The pall that hung over Ford Motor Co. and other non-conforming early automakers was the Selden patent, ironically illustrated by the placements of these two ads in a popular magazine of 1904. The Association of Licensed Automobile Mfrs. was a Selden patent monopoly which sued Ford late in 1903 in an attempt to collect royalties or force him out of business. Ford resisted, but it took until early 1909 for the case to be heard and, initially, the Selden patent was validated. Ford was so downhearted he considered selling out to Billy Durant's General Motors. If that had happened, there would have been no Chevrolet and the end of Ford Motor Co. An appeals court reversed the decision in 1911, however, and the licensing monopoly decided to drop the matter since the patent only had another year to run. The way was cleared for Ford and other carmakers to proceed without legal fears. This opened the floodgates for Ford's mass-production. (N)

After a hiccup in 1904–1905, Ford production skyrocketed from some 1,700 cars in 1903 to industry leadership with 8,800 in 1906 and on to 18,000 in 1909 with the Model T. The Piquette plant could no longer support sales volumes, so the company erected a new plant in Highland Park, then a northern Detroit suburb. The Highland Park plant, shown in this period drawing, for the first time included manufacturing as well as assembly. (D)

Under the guidance of Ford associate James Couzens, much of Ford's success could be attributed to its distribution system, typified here by a view of the company's New York City branch office photographed c. 1910. Ford branches were established across the United States and Canada as well as overseas. (N)

The keystone of the Model T Ford's success was Henry's almost messianic commitment to both low price and, by the standards of the time, reliability. This helped earn sales to fleets such as the New York City Fire Department, whose cars are depicted here in 1911. Maintaining a low price posture in combination with reliability has been an important source of fleet business for Ford through the years. (N)

Although Henry Ford decisively won his Selden patent suit and was then accepted as an industry leader, he remained skittish about fellow automakers. He met with the new National Association of Automobile Manufacturers, as shown here in 1912, but his company nevertheless did not join the successor Automobile Manufacturers Association, long dominated by General Motors, until 1956. (N)

By 1912, Ford production had climbed ten-fold in only three years—to 170,000 at the new Highland Park Plant—but still could not meet demand. Henry Ford's men began devising ways to expedite the production of all components. That culminated in the moving final assembly line shown here at Highland Park late in 1913, the year Ford's U.S. production was 203,000. In comparison, GM turned out only 27,000 of its volume car, Buick, that year. (N)

By the end of 1913, Highland Park could produce 1,000 Model T Fords daily, more than a half-year's output in its first three years just a decade earlier. This view shows Model Ts lined up outside the Highland Park plant for a publicity photograph. Ford Motor Company has been astute throughout the years in its use of publicity and advertising. (P)

When Ford's Highland Park plant opened in 1910 as the company's first integrated manufacturing and assembly facility, it was state-of-the-art in U.S. factory design. Sharing Woodward Avenue frontage with the administration building and showroom in this c. 1915 photo was the powerhouse (left). Powerhouses were typical focal points of large-scale Ford industrial landscapes, while water storage tanks with Ford signage marked many smaller facilities. (S)

In 1914, at a time when most workers earned far less, Ford changed its pay scale from $2.34 for a 9-hour day to $5 for an 8-hour day. Thousands of men came to Detroit from all over the world seeking jobs working on Model Ts like this unrestored 1915 or 1916 model (not a "1914" as the sign says), pictured at the auto industry's Golden Jubilee in 1946. (R)

As economies of scale evolved from mass production, Ford reduced prices, reaching two milestones in 1915, when these coast-to-coast adventurers visited Highland Park. The one millionth Ford was built on December 10, and total North American production exceeded 500,000 for the year. Although people think of the T as unchanging, by now it was mounting electric lights and soon would abandon the brass radiator. (S)

This is a typical Ford branch assembly plant and sales office. It opened in 1915 in Louisville, Kentucky, and was the first of four assembly facilities there, two of which still operate today. It was less expensive then to ship parts to regional plants for final assembly. Such plants also provided both quicker deliveries to dealers and a local presence good for public relations. (W)

Two other seminal events took place in 1915: the completion of Henry and Clara's new home, Fair Lane estate along the Rouge River in Dearborn (above), and the announcement of a huge plant to be built downstream on the same meandering river. By this time, the Dodge brothers, long-time major suppliers as well as Ford stockholders, had started their own auto company, and Henry was chafing at rebellious minority stockholders like the Dodges. (S)

Henry promised to mass-produce "Eagle" subchasers for the Navy during World War I, partly to help build the new Rouge complex. The first ship produced at the government-financed plant is pictured here late in 1918. After the war, Henry purchased the plant and proceeded to fulfill his vision of total control over production, from raw materials to finished car, a process called vertical integration. The Rouge became the world's largest industrial complex. (D)

Automobile manufacturers grew able to produce more specialized vehicles than their initial simple runabouts. Among the most significant was Ford's first truck, the Model TT shown here, introduced in 1917. In order to carry cargo, it was built with a heavier frame, longer wheelbase, and heftier running gear than a Model T passenger car. (W)

Henry achieved his goal of making life easier for the farmer in 1917 with introduction of the Fordson farm tractor, shown here on a Georgia farm. The Fordson was only distantly related to the Model T and was rushed into production as part of the war effort. It formed the basis of an extensive worldwide farm and commercial tractor business over ensuing decades. (W)

Four

ROUGE PLANT
WORLD'S LARGEST
INDUSTRIAL COMPLEX

1916–PRESENT

Of all the operations conducted within Ford Motor Company's Rouge complex—"The World's Largest Industrial City," none is more typical of Henry's vertical integration concept than steel production. Nor are any of the diverse industries inside its fences more capital-intensive. Plant facilities dedicated to steel-making included coke ovens, blast furnaces for the reduction of iron ore, open-hearth furnaces for converting pig iron to steel, and rolling mills for producing the final product. In later years the Ford Steel Division was updated to include a basic oxygen furnace and continuous casting facilities. Unable to stay competitive while paying autoworker's wages, the company spun-off its steel operations in 1981 as Rouge Steel Company, then sold the entire business, including steel-processing plants within the Rouge, to outside investors in 1989. Thus ended a long-standing Henry Ford legacy. (W)

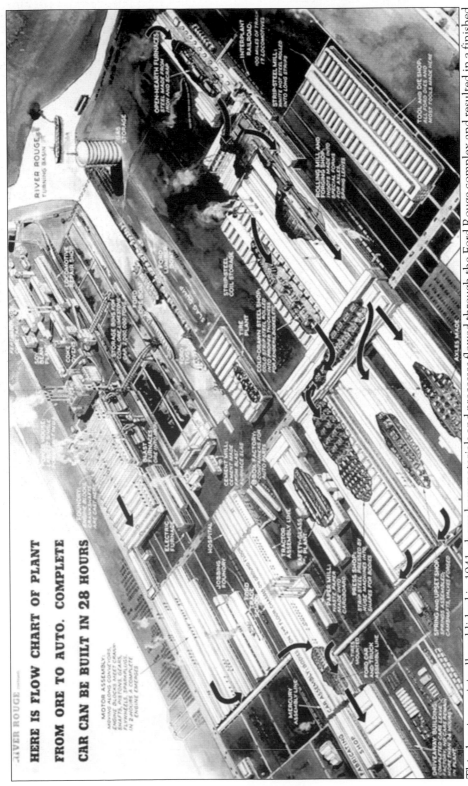

This drawing, originally published in 1941, shows how materials and processes flowed through the Ford Rouge complex and resulted in a finished automobile within 28 hours of raw materials arriving at the docks. Although more than 60 years have passed since the illustration was created, much of what is depicted remains valid today. (N)

Development of the Ford Rouge Plant site had been underway for nearly 15 years when this aerial photograph was taken in 1931. Many of the 1,200 acres remained empty, particularly the area just west of the boat slip (at right), because major development was then concentrated in steel-making operations east of the slip and in vehicle production along Road 4, the complex's major east-west axis. (N)

This 1936 vintage nighttime photo gives poignant testimony to the 24-hour operation that has characterized the Ford Rouge for most of its 87 years. The ship in the foreground is the *Benson Ford*, one of the company's original ore-carrying Great Lakes vessels. The truss-like structure directly ahead of the ship extending to the boat slip was the heart of the raw-material unloading system that fed adjacent stockpiles. (W)

Shown here in the foreground are stockpiles of raw materials essential to production of iron and steel at the Rouge: coal, iron ore, and limestone. The elevated track behind them, called the High Line, fed these ingredients to the blast furnaces at middle left. Also prominent are the eight silver-grey stacks of the Ford powerhouse, which at one time generated enough electricity to power a medium-sized city. (W)

Located directly south of the powerhouse and east of the High Line were the coke ovens. Here coal from Appalachia was converted to hotter-burning coke which, when burned with iron ore and limestone in the blast furnaces, produced pig iron. Some of this iron was converted to steel for automotive stampings and frames. The rest was used in Rouge foundries for casting engine parts, transmission cases, and axle housings. (R)

Open-hearth furnaces, once the heart of Ford's steel-making operations inside the Rouge, converted pig iron from the blast furnaces into steel ingots. The ingots were transferred on railway flatcars to the nearby rolling mill where they were progressively "squeezed" to various thicknesses appropriate for stamping into body panels and chassis components. (R)

Manufacturing engines was another key operation within the Rouge complex. Pictured here are hundreds of recently completed 1936 vintage Ford V-8 engines. The powertrain assemblies (engine, clutch, and transmission) to the left were being electrically "motored" to ensure that all internal components moved freely. (W)

Body stamping was a relative newcomer to Rouge activities when this photo was taken right after World War II. Prior to 1938, when what was then the world's largest stamping plant opened here, Ford body assemblies were provided by outside firms: Briggs Manufacturing Company, The Budd Company and Murray Corporation of America. This particular operation is forming top panels for Ford and Mercury sedans. (R)

In keeping with Henry Ford's philosophy of vertically integrated manufacturing, Ford was the only automotive manufacturer to both produce and fabricate its own glass. Operations were located initially at the Rouge and in St. Paul, Minnesota, where Ford's assembly and glass plant was erected near a sandpit. Subsequent glass plants were built in Nashville, Tennessee, Tulsa, Oklahoma, and Niagara Falls, Ontario. When Ford created Visteon Corporation in 2000 for its former component supply operations, it included Glass Division in the spin-off. (W)

Despite his long-time friendship with Harvey Firestone, Henry Ford elected to add tire manufacture to the company's activities, and in 1938 he opened a state-of-the-art plant within the Rouge. This plant made tires for Ford cars as well as specialized tires for farm tractors. After the facility closed in 1942, Ford's tire-making machinery was sent to the Soviet Union through the government's Lend-Lease program. (W)

Production of vehicles, such as these 1953 Fords, signified the culmination of Ford's vertical integration. Vehicle assembly started at the Rouge in late 1927 with the first Model As. Originally the "B Building," home of the Eagle Boats, the facility has been called "Dearborn Assembly" or "DAP" for decades and has been the sole source of Mustang production for many years. (N)

Left: By-products of vertical integration were an important Ford activity and not limited to the Rouge. The Charcoal Briquets illustrated in this advertisement, for example, were produced before World War II at the company's wood-processing facilities in Michigan's Upper Peninsula. (W)

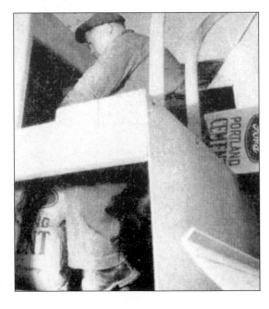

Right: Portland Cement was another Ford by-product directly tied to the Rouge. It was made from blast furnace slag that resulted from iron-making operations and was primarily used within the company for new construction. By-product bags of cement, charcoal, and fertilizer were sold to employees. (W)

The major automakers approached co-op education differently: Ford to high-school-plus technical training, General Motors Institute to undergraduate engineering degrees, and Chrysler Institute, master's degrees. Henry Ford's Trade School, founded in 1916, trained 8,000 machinists, draftsmen, and other skilled engineering and manufacturing workers before it was folded into the United Auto Workers apprentice program in 1952. Here, Ford Trade School students labor on drafting boards in the Rouge in the 1930s. (W)

In 1941 the company established the Ford Navy Service School at the Rouge plant and leased it to the government for a dollar a year. Instructors from the Trade School put classes of 2,000 sailors at a time through three months' intensive training in mechanical and technical subjects, including ship maintenance and aircraft engine repair. (R)

This c. 1937 view of Rouge parking lots along Miller Road at the east side of the complex shows how typical Ford workers commuted. Although private cars for such transportation were not as universally accepted then, the huge number of Rouge workers' cars always amazed foreign visitors. Equally significant is the electric streetcar moving through its turnaround and pickup station in the right foreground. Detroit's Department of Street Railways ran an extensive trolley schedule to accommodate Ford workers. During World War II, when gas and tires were rationed, this public transit system proved its worth. The eight stacks of the Rouge powerhouse in the background help orient the parking lots to other images in this chapter. (N)

Throngs of Ford workers move toward Gate 4, the main exit, on their way to parking lots and bus stops during a shift change in 1955. Buildings of interest along Road 4 are the long-ago-razed Motor Assembly at the immediate right, Dearborn Assembly next right, the electric furnace building beyond railroad cars at left, and the stamping plant crossing over the road in the distance. (N)

Ford was a pioneer and long-time leader in social programs for its workers. The company provided employment to handicapped individuals such as these blind men, who are shown in 1941 performing an assembly operation involving small parts. Using the skills of all available workers became especially crucial during the war years. (R)

Henry and Edsel Ford, aided by a scale model, are shown here discussing the proposed Naval Training Station at the Rouge with U.S. Navy officials. The school was built and opened in 1941 and served the Navy Department for the war's duration. The Station was located adjacent to the Rouge ship turn-around basin and included classrooms, a recreation center, and eight barracks. (W)

This 1936 aerial view of the Rouge shows changes from the 1931 view on page 35. The new Rotunda visitor reception center is in the foreground. To its left, across Schaefer Road, is Ford's Administration Building. Beyond that, Detroit, Toledo, and Ironton rail yards serve the Rouge complex in the background. Note, in this pre-natural-gas era, the two huge cylindrical holders for manufactured gas. At its peaks, Rouge employment exceeded 100,000. (N)

Five

DISTRACTIONS

1915–1945

In 1915 Henry Ford, well on his way to becoming "The Last Billionaire," began what would become a 30-year series of endeavors unrelated to the core car, truck, and tractor manufacturing business. Except for his tacit support of anti-Semitic writings—despite having Jewish friends and business associates upon whom he depended—in a Ford-owned broadsheet in the 1920s, most of these quixotic missions were good-hearted even if wrong-headed. Here he is shown on the Peace Ship he underwrote in 1915 for a fruitless voyage to end the war in Europe. Ford's encouragement of a Sociology Department to teach immigrant worker families how to cope with urban American life was short-lived, and his campaign for election to the U.S. Senate on the Democratic ticket in 1918 was unsuccessful. (S)

Henry Ford Hospital in Detroit, shown here in 1920, became the longest lasting and one of the most significant of Henry Ford's non-automotive ventures. He began underwriting the hospital's cost in 1909, oversaw its design, and watched it grow into one of the nation's leading teaching hospitals, even though it lacked direct university affiliation. (H)

When Henry began expanding the Rouge into an industrial colossus after World War I, he found that bridges blocked access for large ore ships. He bought the bankrupt Detroit, Toledo & Ironton Railroad so he could replace a key bridge, not only clearing the way for ships but also turning the coal and passenger carrier into a successful rail line, which he sold at a profit in only a few years. Shown here is the Delray station near the plant. (G)

Henry's personal wealth accumulated rapidly thanks to the Model T, allowing him to become interested in the rich man's pastime, yachting. He bought a 201-foot yacht in 1916 for sailing the Great Lakes. Here he is shown in a yachtsman's cap in the 1920s. (R)

Ford ordered two 612-foot ore-carriers, completed in 1924, as an early step to control the flow of raw materials to the new Rouge plant. This is the flagship *Henry Ford II*, whose sister ship was the *Benson Ford*. These freighters toted iron ore from Ford mines along Lake Superior to Dearborn. Ford also bought coal mines and lumber reserves to supply Rouge production. (D)

Henry also envisioned an ocean-going fleet to carry Ford vehicles and parts from Michigan to the rest of the world. The company bought more than 200 war-surplus ships, mostly freighters sized to pass from the Lakes into the Atlantic. Most were cut up for scrap, as shown here, but some were put to work in the Ford Fleet. (R)

Top: In an ingenious move, Ford gutted 13 of the surplus freighters, converting them to barges to be towed through the Great Lakes by Ford tugs as shown here. They carried raw materials as well as vehicle parts. (D)

Middle: Another type of Ford ship was the canal vessel, designed with low superstructure to ply New York's canal system in operations between Dearborn and the East Coast. The *Chester,* shown here departing the Rouge with 1933-model vehicles on its deck, was one of four ordered by Ford in the 1930s. (R)

Bottom: The *Lake Osweya,* pictured here in New York harbor *c.*1938, was typical of the ocean freighters in Ford's fleet of 30-plus vessels. In February 1942, it became the first of five Ford ships sunk by German submarines during World War II. Two other Ford ships sank in raging ocean storms. At war's end, Ford abandoned all but its two large lake-going ore carriers. (D)

48

During the 1920s, Detroit aspired to become the aviation—as well as automotive—capital of the world. Ford's contributions were many: best known is the famous Ford Tri-Motor all-metal passenger plane shown here. It was produced in assembly-line fashion in factories set up on the edge of a new Ford airport in Dearborn. More than 170 Tri-Motors were built and sold between 1926 and 1932. (N)

Ford also experimented with this single-place "Flying Flivver," shown with comedian Will Rogers in the cockpit. (Model T Fords were popularly known as "flivvers" and "tin lizzies"). The plan died when Ford's test pilot perished in a crash of one of two Flivvers off the Florida coast in 1928. Within a few years, the air was filled with inexpensive small training planes, mostly built in Ohio and Pennsylvania by companies other than Ford. (D)

In addition to supporting the Tri-Motor business, Ford created the first commercial air service from the Ford airport, and the first airport hotel, Dearborn Inn, seen in the left foreground in 1930. At the top are Henry Ford Museum and Greenfield Village, started in 1929 and destined to become Michigan's leading tourist attraction—and Henry's leading distraction in his later years. (P)

Henry Ford began hiring large numbers of African-Americans for his Detroit-area plants as early as 1914, long before most industrialists. His friendship with Tuskegee Institute plant scientist George Washington Carver, shown here in the 1930s with Edsel Ford and Henry, was concentrated however on agricultural matters, especially the development of soybeans for industrial applications. (N)

Henry planted many acres of soybeans on his Dearborn farms, and pushed development of soybean-based plastics. This is the soybean processing plant erected at the Rouge in the 1930s. Soybean-based plastics made it into pre-war Ford cars as window and control knobs, but lacked durability. The project would not have lasted as long as it did without Henry's involvement. (W)

The height of Henry's effort to convert farm products for industrial use was this experimental car with soybean-plastic body panels over a tubular steel frame. It was unveiled in August 1941 not long before America's entry into war. At that time, plastic panels proved infeasible for mass production. Plastic bodies were not successfully mass-produced until Chevrolet introduced fiberglass bodies for the 1953 Corvette. (R)

Ford began converting old water mills into small parts-producing factories in the 1920s. One example was this Northville, Michigan, valve plant. The program was contrary to principles of low-cost mass production, but fitted with Henry's rural background and his goal of making factory employment convenient for farmers. He also appreciated water power. (W)

Another such "village industry" was the Flat Rock plant, southwest of metropolitan Detroit, where a small Ford factory produced automobile headlamps, as shown here. Most of Ford's water-side "village" industries were located in southeastern Michigan, but exceptions included some in urban areas, including Green Island, New York, near Albany, and the Twin Cities assembly plant in St. Paul, which still operates today as one of Ford's oldest and best plants. (R)

When steel replaced wood in automobile bodies in the 1930s, Ford's vast forest preserves in Michigan's Upper Peninsula were no longer needed. Yet, Henry created this "model" lumber mill town in Alberta in the late 1930s, ostensibly as an experiment and to create employment, but really as something of a hobby. Ford Motor Company donated the property to Michigan Technological University for its Forestry program in 1954. (R)

Six

BUSINESS AS USUAL

1921–1931

In this photograph, 64-year-old Henry Ford is affixing motor number "A1" to the first production engine of the new Ford Model A, symbolizing Ford Motor Company's major event of the 1920s. In May 1927, Ford shut down U.S. production of Model T cars after assembling its "15 millionth," pictured on page 56. It was not until November 1, 1927 that the company completed changeover from the "T" to the "A" and resumed production of cars. During that five-month halt in output, dealers and workers suffered lost income and Ford lost industry leadership to General Motors. The Model T's replacement was named in honor of the company's first vehicle: the 1903 Model A. The new "A" established an outstanding record for reliability and was renowned for economical operation. One highly-regarded business historian said of it: "Dollar for dollar, pound for pound the Ford Model A was the best car ever built!" When trade restrictions arose at the end of the decade, forcing Ford to develop smaller cars for European markets, the Model A became Ford's last singular world car, successful in all markets, until the end of the century. The clutch and brake pedals in the photo remind us that the new Ford had a conventional three-speed sliding-gear transmission in place of the then-obsolete planetary transmission of the Model T. (R)

Henry Ford purchased the bankrupt Lincoln Motor Company, a builder of high-quality automobiles, for $8 million on February 4, 1922. Pictured following the sale in Lincoln's Detroit headquarters are Henry M. Leland, Lincoln founder; Mrs. Edsel Ford; Edsel Ford; Mrs. Henry Ford; Henry Ford; Mrs. Wilfred Leland, and Henry Leland's son, Wilfred, a Lincoln official. A portrait of Abraham Lincoln, after whom the company was named, hangs on the wall. (W)

Lincoln Motor Company was located at Warren and Livernois Avenues in Detroit. Production started here in September 1920 and continued until end of the 1952 model year. Known within Ford as the Lincoln Plant, this building served as headquarters for that company and its successor, Lincoln-Mercury Division, until 1955. Following a divisional split, it became Mercury headquarters. In 1957 it was sold to Detroit Edison and torn down in 2002. (N)

When Ford purchased Lincoln in 1922, custom-bodied models—such as this Brunn Town Car on a huge 136-inch wheelbase—typified luxury cars. The early Lincoln's quality was impeccable, and its engineering, especially its L-head V-8 engine with a 60-degree bank angle, was unique. Lincoln production was minuscule by Ford standards: a mere 5,512 Lincolns were created during the first year of ownership, when well over a million Model Ts were turned out. (W)

In 1923 Ford Motor Company constructed this sprawling Engineering Laboratory in Dearborn. It was used for nearly all design and development, including styling, until the early 1950s. Ford Airport and the buildings for manufacturing Tri-Motor airplanes are shown in the background of this c. 1928 photo. The empty land between the lab and airport would soon be used for construction of Henry Ford Museum and Greenfield Village. (N)

Although many people thought the Model T, five million of which had been produced by 1921, was unchanging, this photograph demonstrates otherwise. This 4,999,999th twist on the usual milestone car shows modifications made in 1917: black radiator shell, new hood, and a smoother cowl-to-body transition. In 1919 an optional electric starter had become available. (W)

Henry Ford posed in 1924 with his 10 millionth car and his Quadricycle. More changes had been made to the "T" by then, notably a higher radiator and hood. The letter "L" on the hood side was the symbol of the Lincoln Highway Association, an outgrowth of the "Good Roads" movement started by bicyclists in the 1890s. (N)

Ford's 15 millionth vehicle went down the line at Highland Park on May 26, 1927. It was among the last Model Ts built in America. Further modifications had been made to the "unchanging car": a more integrated and color-lacquered body, bar-mounted headlamps, nickel-plated radiator shell, and wire-spoke wheels. In only six years, Ford had built 10 million cars. (R)

When Ford's Highland Park plant opened in 1910, it was considered an outstanding example of modern industrial architecture, a tribute to Albert Kahn's genius. Over the years Highland Park has served as "Home of the Model T," a truck plant, a tractor plant, a parts plant, and a depository for company records. The property was sold in 1981 and today the remaining buildings appear neglected and forgotten. (N)

This 1920s dealership symbolizes the importance of the dealer organization to the success of Ford Motor Company. Ford's dealers sold and serviced Model Ts, Fordson tractors, and Lincolns. By absorbing overproduction in 1921, they allowed Henry Ford to avoid borrowing money. But, dissatisfied by 1927's production hiatus for changeover to the Model A, many shifted allegiance to Chevrolet. (S)

By 1925 Ford was producing complete trucks, rather than just the One-Ton Chassis of 1917. This example was equipped with an open cab and the recently announced platform body with stake racks. Note the kerosene side lamps and heavy-duty truck rear wheels and tires. (N)

Middle: In a mid-1920s quest for new types of cross-country command-and-reconnaissance vehicles, the U.S. Army evaluated numerous prototypes at Aberdeen Proving Ground. This example, based on the Model T. Ford, would be involved with military vehicles, directly or indirectly, over the next 40 years. (N)

Bottom: Ford's first light-duty pickup truck was announced on April 15, 1925, and consisted of an optional body for the Runabout car model. It attached to the chassis in place of the standard rear deck. De-mountable rim wheels were an option for quick tire changes at a time when punctures were common. (W)

Known to a generation of Ford people as "3000 Schaefer Road," this Dearborn structure was tagged the Administration Building when it opened in 1928. A modest-sized building compared to General Motors' contemporary skyscraper offices, it served as Ford Motor Company headquarters until 1956. Then it became home to the Lincoln Division and later the re-united Lincoln-Mercury Division. Its last tenant prior to being razed in 1997 was the Ford Parts and Service Division. (D)

Shown under construction in 1930, the Ford Edgewater Plant was located opposite New York City in New Jersey. Intended to serve New York, New Jersey and European export markets (note the dock facilities), the plant never reached its international potential due to the Great Depression and aftereffects of World War II. Edgewater operated until 1955 when a sprawling plant in Mahwah, New Jersey, replaced it. (N)

The transfer of car production from Highland Park to the Rouge with the new Model A of 1928 was another milestone for Ford. The black, rather than nickel-plated, radiator shell on the second Model A chassis on the line in this 1929 picture at the Rouge identifies it as a commercial model intended for a pickup or panel delivery body later in the assembly process. (R)

One of the first tasks undertaken by Edsel Ford as president of Lincoln Motor Company in 1922 was enhancing the cars' aesthetics. He engaged the leading custom body builders of the Classic era. Among the most creative of these was LeBaron, whose distinctly styled Aero Phaeton is depicted here on a 1929 Model L chassis. The name reflected the contemporary passion for aviation. (W)

Members of the Edsel Ford family posed for this informal portrait, probably at Henry and Clara's Fair Lane estate, during the summer of 1929. From left, they are Benson, William Clay, Edsel, Josephine, Eleanor and Henry Ford II. At that time Edsel would have been 35 years old, Henry nearly 12, Benson 9, and William Clay 4. (P)

Three of Edsel Ford's children are shown in their "toy" English automobiles at their Gaulkler Pointe estate in 1930. Henry II is behind the wheel of an MG M-type with Benson at his side. Their sister Josephine is seated in her half-size car inspired by the "Bullnose" Morris Cowley. Interestingly, the Morris Cowley is sometimes credited with "stealing" the British market from the Model T. (N)

Henry Ford drove the 20 millionth Ford, a Model A Town Sedan, from Rouge Assembly on April 14, 1931. This car was both a milestone and one of three new slant-windshield sedans introduced in 1931, a re-style which would be the Model A's last. In the U.S., the last "As" were commercial chassis built in December 1932, but the hardy models were assembled elsewhere in the world until 1936. (R)

This *Detroit News* photo of workers leaving Ford's Highland Park plant was taken in January 1929, months before the stock market crash and while the domestic economy was still booming. Ford did have temporary work stoppages that year and this might have been one of them. The workers' downcast looks suggest what was to come during the Great Depression. (R)

Seven

DEPRESSION YEARS, FAMILY AND UNION SQUABBLES, AND WORLD WAR II

1932–1945

A photographer captured Edsel Ford and his father Henry in avid discourse sometime in the 1930s. Edsel, a gentleman in the best sense, was named president of Ford Motor Company in 1919 at age 25 but his dominating father always overshadowed him. Edsel pressed his father to modernize the company and its products at every opportunity. Henry became more obstinate with age and delayed replacement of the Model T, ignored the medium-price market that led to great successes by General Motors and the new Chrysler Corporation, and held onto mechanical brakes long after competitors had adopted hydraulics. Henry Ford, nearly 70 at the company's 30th Anniversary in 1933, increasingly relied on his Rouge enforcer, Harry Bennett, for operating policies. Consequently, Ford fell from its place as industry sales leader in 1926—to third place after GM and Chrysler—by 1933. (N)

The Lincoln car in particular—and design in general—were Edsel's havens throughout the difficult years of being suppressed by his father. Here is Edsel at the wheel of a 1932 Lincoln V-12 roadster pace car at the annual Indianapolis 500 race. In racing, at least, he found common ground with his testy father. (N)

Beginning in the late 1920s, protective trade barriers and related "horsepower taxes" aimed at American imports compelled Ford (and GM) to develop unique small cars for production and sale in Britain and Germany. This is the English Ford Model Y, which resembles a miniature U.S. 1933 Ford. (W)

American production of the Model A Ford ended in 1932 after a four-year run. It lived on in Russia, however, after Henry sold parts, plans, and tooling to the Soviet Union and sent experts to help set up two plants. Here Ford touring cars, called "GAZ-As" by the Russians, are being produced in a Soviet factory c. 1933. Ford quit sending them parts in 1934 after the Soviets reneged on paying their bills. (W)

The Greatest Value in the History of the Automobile

New Ford Eight De Luxe Tudor Sedan

THE NEW FORD EIGHT is the greatest value ever offered Canadian motorists. It is so new and different — so far ahead in design and performance — that there is no basis for comparison.

There has never been a car like the New Ford Eight. None with such a perfect balance of speed, power, comfort, ease of control and economy. None that so completely fulfills every motoring desire. None so altogether pleasing to every member of the family.

Words just can't begin to describe the regard and enthusiasm you'll have for the New Ford Eight. The very first time you drive it, you will say that you have never known an automobile at any price that put so much joy and satisfaction in motoring. When you buy the New Ford Eight you buy more than a new eight-cylinder automobile. You buy a wholly new kind of automobile. It creates a wholly new standard of value and performance in a low-price car.

See the remarkable New Ford Eight and the New Ford Four at the showrooms of the nearest Ford dealer and arrange for a demonstration. Take the wheel yourself for an amazing new thrill in motoring.

FEATURES OF THE NEW FORD EIGHT

Low, roomy bodies, attractively finished. Soft, comfortable seats. The smooth, vibrationless performance of a 65-horsepower eight-cylinder engine. Rapid acceleration. 75 miles an hour in high. Silent second gear. Silent synchronized gear shift. Automatic spark control. Down-draft carburetor and silencer. Easy-riding springs and self-adjusting Houdaille shock absorbers, with thermostatic control. Exceptionally low gasoline and oil consumption. Safety glass windshield in all body types. Safety glass throughout in Sport Coupe, Cabriolet, Victoria, Convertible Sedan and all De Luxe cars.

"The Canadian Car"

THE NEW FORD EIGHT

The big news of 1932, when auto industry sales dipped to one-third of the 1928 level, was the March introduction of the Ford Eight, promoted in this Canadian advertisement. Production of the basic chassis, called "platform" today, continued until 1948 and the flat-head V-8 engine until 1953. (W)

In celebration of Ford Motor Company's 30th Anniversary, Henry Ford posed in a restored 1903 Model A beside a horse-drawn carriage. In only a couple of decades, Ford cars had effectively replaced such centuries-old conveyances. (R)

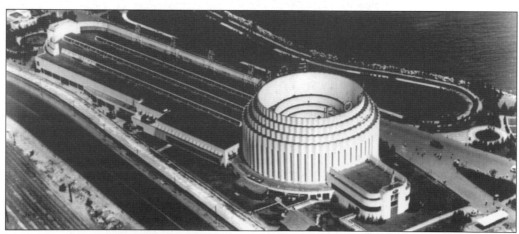

Ford commissioned the gear-shaped Rotunda building for its exhibit at Chicago's 1934 World's Fair. It was later moved to Dearborn where it became a visitor center for Rouge tours and factory delivery of new cars. Several Rotunda replicas were built, including one for the 1935 San Diego Exposition, which is now an aerospace museum. (S)

Auto companies were fond of promoting milestone vehicles. Here Henry and Edsel watch in 1934 as the body is lowered to the chassis of the one millionth V-8. The event also symbolized industry recovery from the Depression. The speedy performance of this vintage Ford prompted outlaw Clyde Barrow to write a testimonial letter to Ford about his favorite "getaway car." (R)

Ford built ten sleek Miller-Ford V-8-powered front-drive racers for the 1935 Indy 500 Race. They shared front-end styling with 1935 Ford passenger cars. Ford dealers loved the promotion. Unfortunately, it was a last-minute rush job: the cars were ill-prepared and untested, the hastily-devised steering gear was defective, and—despite the last-minute adjustments pictured—none of the qualifiers finished the race. (D)

Ford finally broke into the medium-price field late in 1935 with this streamlined Lincoln-Zephyr V-12. U.S. Lincoln registrations leaped twelve-fold from 2,100 in 1934 to 25,200 in 1937, a period when still-recovering industry sales increased 84 percent. The new junior Lincoln was popular overseas, too. This photo was taken in Brazil. The Zephyr was considered a personal triumph for Edsel. (W)

With Ford's aviation ventures abandoned—at least until World War II—the company decided in 1937 to convert its Dearborn "Ford Field" airport to a close-at-hand automotive test track. The Tri-Motor airframe building and hangers became experimental garages. This illustration shows some of the proving ground features built into the one-time airfield. Notably, the main runway became a high-speed track. (W)

Undeterred by fears rising from the Lindbergh kidnapping only a few years before, the Edsel Ford family posed outside their Gaulkler Pointe estate on Lake St. Clair about 1937. Left to right are Edsel (1893–1943), wife Eleanor Clay (1896–1976), Henry II (1917–1987), Benson (1919–1978), Josephine (1923–) and William Clay (1925–). At the time, Young Henry was a student at Yale and Benson was headed to Princeton. (N)

Ford built its 25 millionth car in January 1937, six years after the 20 millionth. It had taken only three years to go from the 10 to the 15 millionth in the mid-1920s when Ford sold more than half the cars made by the industry. These milestone cars were typically dispatched to tour dealerships, state fairs, and other events around the country. (R)

Top: Ford assembled its first cars in Great Britain in 1911 and started manufacturing there in 1912. Because of this early start, Britain has been Ford's strongest European market. After the 1931 completion of the huge Dagenham plant near London—where this fashionable pre-war English Ford was built—Fords made in the UK were distinctive models designed for the local and Empire markets. (N)

Middle: Ford Motor Company of France entered a joint venture with the French Mathis Company, which produced this Matford V-8 before World War II. It bears only slight resemblance to U.S. Ford V-8s of the time. (N)

Bottom: In order to meet German government requirements and produce a unique Ford for the German market, the company established a manufacturing and assembly plant in Cologne in 1931, where cars like this custom-bodied 1939 Cabriolet V-8 were built. (N)

In the fall of 1938, Henry and Edsel joined the press and dealers at the Dearborn Test Track for introduction of the 1939 Mercury, Ford Motor Company's new entry in the lower-middle price range. With a body and V-8 engine larger than the Ford's, Mercury jumped to instant success with annual sales over 80,000. It was noted for being exceptionally quiet for cars of the time. (R)

The "big" Lincoln Model K was phased out in 1939–1940 because its sales had declined to a few hundred a year. When Mercury was introduced, dealerships that specialized in Mercury and Lincoln-Zephyr sales and service began to form, such as this Washington state facility displaying 1939 models. The Lincoln-Mercury Division as such was not organized until after World War II.

According to legend, Edsel Ford had this custom "Continental" version of a 1939 Lincoln-Zephyr convertible created specifically for his winter vacation in Florida in 1939. It resulted in such interest that it was hastily advanced to limited production of both convertible and coupe versions for 1940 models. A new classic was born. The car's influence on design and its boost to Ford prestige were lasting. (W)

Edsel and Eleanor, shown here arriving for their son Benson's wedding in 1941, also had the chauffeur-driven, Brunn-bodied Lincoln limousine seen in the background. After Edsel's death, Mrs. Ford arranged for the Brunn body to be transferred to later-model Lincolns and used it until her death in 1976. Mr. and Mrs. Ford were patrons of the arts, and those arts extended to custom cars. (R)

This Brunn-bodied 1939 Lincoln Model K convertible sedan was made for the President of the United States. Before World War II, custom-body manufacturers prospered, building such special designs on conventional luxury-car frames. Their businesses largely evaporated in the post-war period. This car, however, was the first in a 50-year-long string of custom Lincolns commissioned by the Secret Service for the White House. (W)

Three years later, the Secret Service had Ford "update" the White House car by grafting a 1942 Lincoln-Zephyr front end to the 1939 Brunn body. President Franklin D. Roosevelt frequently used it as an open parade limousine before and during World War II. It became known as "Sunshine Special." (W)

The versatility of Ford assembly plants in the pre-war period is illustrated in this photograph of the Dearborn facility's drive-away area. The variety of vehicles it produced included Ford trucks (upper left), all models of 1940 Ford passenger cars (center), and 1940 Mercurys (right). In the post-war period, production generally became much more specialized, with separate facilities devoted to each type of vehicle. (N)

Photographs of the first three generations of the Ford Dynasty together as adults are rare. Here are "Young Henry," "Old Henry," and Edsel, in a photo probably taken at the New York Auto Show in January 1941, the same time and location as the photo on page 4. At this time, Henry II had been on the company payroll only a few months. (F)

Production of Ford farm tractors had moved back and forth between two U.S. locations and two in the British Isles over the 20-plus years since the introduction of the Fordson tractor in 1917. This photograph of Henry on the famous Model 9N tractor with an admiring lad alongside him was taken in 1939 when the 9N was introduced. (R)

Ford's first buses were based on front-engined Model AA truck chassis, and were used interchangeably for school and transit service. In the early 1940s, the company introduced this rear-engined bus specifically designed for transit service. Co-author Michael W.R. Davis recalls riding in such V-8-powered buses in his hometown of Louisville, Kentucky, during World War II. GM came to dominate the post-war bus market with its diesel-powered units. (W)

Left: Few of the thousands of photographs of Henry Ford show him smiling and having a good time, but here he is with son Edsel and entertainer Will Rogers (left) at a 1934 World Series baseball game in Detroit. (R)

Right: The third generation of Fords also enjoyed being spectators at sports events. Here Henry Ford II and his new bride, Anne, are shown at another Detroit Tigers baseball game, September 18, 1940. (R)

Ford shared with Willys-Overland the production order from the U.S. Army for quarter-ton general-purposes (GP) vehicles, which GIs came to call "Jeeps" (a name later trade-marked by Willys). Here Edsel drives the first Ford prototype GP, then labelled "Blitz Buggy," off the line on February 28, 1941. Ford built 278,000 GPs during the war. (R)

When the United Auto Workers set out to organize the auto industry in the 1930s, Ford became the lone holdout, fighting the union all the way to the U.S. Supreme Court. The UAW finally prevailed and, after an April 1941 strike, Ford capitulated. Here women and children sympathy pickets are shown outside the Rouge plant. (R)

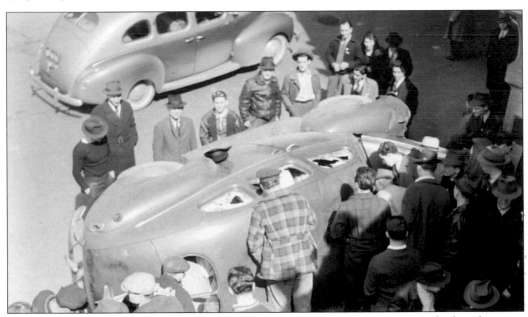

At issue for workers were seniority rights and orderly settlement of grievances, which only union representation appeared capable of resolving. The strike was highly emotional for both workers and strikers, and resulted in violence outside the Rouge plant. Here a car was apparently battered and overturned by UAW pickets blocking non-strikers from reaching their jobs. (R)

Left: Benson Ford is shown getting a head start on World War II as he was being processed at the Army induction center at Fort Wayne in Detroit, June 14, 1941. He ended the war as a captain in the Army Air Corps. (R)

Right: By fall 1941, long before the Pearl Harbor attack, Henry Ford II had been commissioned into the Navy. Here he is shown in his Ensign's uniform with wife Anne, October 27, 1941. (R)

Edsel Ford died unexpectedly on May 26, 1943, leaving his aged father in charge. The U.S. government feared adverse affects on war production and released Henry II from the Navy to return to Ford Motor Company. He's shown here in 1944 with Rouge chief Harry Bennett, a man he had to fire to obtain free reign running the company. (N)

The last civilian Ford passenger car produced after Pearl Harbor was not a Ford as is commonly believed, but rather this right-hand-drive 1942 Mercury sedan assembled in mid-April 1942 at Windsor, Ontario, Canada, for export to Kenya. (W)

Besides GPs, B-24 bombers, aircraft engines, gliders, tanks, tank engines, armored cars and other war material, Ford supported the war effort by producing Army versions of its 1942 trucks, as shown here. Altogether, Ford U.S. built some 413,000 vehicles for the Allied cause. (W)

Ford's most notable wartime achievement was mass-production of B-24 bombers at a new plant at Willow Run, west of Detroit, beginning in 1941. Here workers are shown on June 28, 1945, autographing the final B-24 built: Number 8,685. (R)

Ford of Canada contributed to the war effort differently than the U.S. company, producing trucks such as this to British military specifications. Ford plants in Britain made vehicles such as the tank-like V-8-powered Bren gun carrier. Plants in Axis hands were forced to turn out war materials, mainly trucks, for the Germans and Japanese. (W)

Just as Ford had been last in the industry to cease civilian production, it was also the first to resume it: this carry-over 1942 pickup truck was turned out at the Rouge on May 3, 1945, and designated as Ford's 31 millionth vehicle. (W)

Henry Ford II replaced his grandfather as president of Ford Motor Company on September 21, 1945, and among his ceremonial duties was presenting Ford's (and the industry's) first post-war passenger car to President Harry S. Truman. The car's assembly had actually been completed on July 3, nearly six weeks before the war's end. (D)

Eight

RECOVERY, EXPANSION, AND COMPETITION

1946–1964

In 1952, on the eve of Ford Motor Company's Fiftieth Anniversary, the Ford brothers—Henry II (standing), Benson (right), and William Clay—posed with portraits of their grandfather Henry (left) and father Edsel (right) in the executive conference room at the company's Administration Building. At the time, Henry was company president and was leaning heavily on the counsel of Ernest Breech, later to become chairman of the board, whom he had hired in 1946 from Bendix Aviation, a General Motors affiliate. Benson was vice president and general manager of Lincoln-Mercury Division. William Clay, a former Navy pilot just four years out of Yale, was the recently-named general manager of Special Product operations. The "special product" was the re-born Lincoln Continental that would be designated Continental *Mark II* when introduced in late 1955. William Clay Ford became a company vice president in October 1953 when Special Product operations became Continental Division. Henry later relegated his younger brothers to non-operating assignments. (D)

Top: After World War II there was huge pent-up worldwide demand for new cars and trucks. Indicative of this interest is the group of people gathered on the sidewalk to watch the unloading of new 1946 Fords at an Illinois dealership. (S)

Middle: Henry Ford II drove a Lincoln pace car at the 1946 Indianapolis 500-Mile Race, just as his father had done 14 years earlier. The 1946 race was the first "Indy Classic" since 1941. The Lincoln is a Continental Cabriolet. Its Firestone tires were that era's favorite Speedway brand.

Bottom: The Automotive Industry Golden Jubilee banquet was held in Detroit's gargantuan Masonic Temple in 1946. Pictured at the honoree table are pioneers Edgar L. Apperson, J. Frank Duryea, Henry Ford, George M. Holley, Charles B. King, Frank Kwilinski, George W. Mason, and Lt. Gen. William S. Knudsen. (N)

The top company executives present at this April 1, 1947 meeting are, from left to right, John R. (Jack) Davis, John S. Bugas, Benson Ford, Henry Ford II, Ernest R. Breech, Albert J. Browning, Harold T. Youngren, and Lewis D. Crusoe. Several were hired from General Motors after Henry Ford II became president, and therefore were relatively new to Ford. Company founder Henry Ford died less than a week later. (N)

After Henry Ford's April 7, 1947, death his body lay in state at Greenfield Village. The funeral followed at the Cathedral Church of St. Paul on Woodward Avenue in Detroit. Note the vehicles: a block-long line of Lincoln sedans for mourners in the funeral procession, newsreel camera cars parked perpendicularly in front of the church and, ironically, a 1941 Packard hearse for Henry's last ride. The streetcars provide further historical perspective. (R)

The first all-new postwar Ford car was the 1949 model introduced at dealerships on June 18, 1948. It was the most extensively changed Ford since the Model A superseded the Model T, and featured both an all-new body and styling and a totally redesigned chassis. Visible in this front-end assembly operation is the new independent coil-spring front suspension. (N)

The 1949 Ford was hailed as the handsomest Ford car since 1932. It was received enthusiastically by long-time Ford owners and attracted many first-time buyers. Known historically as "The Car That Saved the Empire" it was also the first Ford since the Model A to sell over one million units during a single model year and, thanks to an 18-month run, outsold all other 1949 makes. (N)

Opposite Top: In addition to the Ford, all of the company's 1949-model North American cars were completely redesigned. The Sport Sedan, shown, and other Mercury body models broke with traditional use of Ford bodies to share a design with a new smaller Lincoln. (N)

Opposite Middle: The Lincoln Cosmopolitan, top series for 1949, was intended for traditional high-priced car buyers, featuring an exclusive family of large bodies. Like the Ford and Mercury, this year's Lincoln adopted a new chassis and a new V-8 engine, its first since 1932. The V-12 was discontinued. (W)

Opposite Bottom: Introduced as part of the all-new 1949 Ford of Canada line, this Meteor was a Ford-based, lower-priced companion to Mercury, sold by Canadian Lincoln-Mercury dealers. Since most Canadian markets could support only one corporate dealership, Ford dealers also sold the Mercury-based Monarch. (W)

Chevrolet's announcement of the Bel Air "hardtop convertible" for 1950 posed a serious threat to Ford's domination of the younger driver market. Unable to bring a comparable model to market quickly enough, in early summer Ford released this Crestliner, a sporty-trimmed Tudor Sedan with fabric-covered roof. (W)

In 1950, Chevrolet was first among the "Low Priced Three" to offer an automatic transmission, Power Glide. Ford countered in 1951 with its own Fordomatic, optional just with V-8s. Ford's "PRNDL" shift pattern became the industry standard under later Federal regulations. (N)

Participation in the Mobilgas Economy Run was viewed as a publicity opportunity by 1950s automakers. In 1951 Lincoln took the top position "Sweepstakes" with over 66 *ton*-miles-per-gallon (miles per gallon adjusted for car weight) while Nash Rambler at 31.05 led in *actual* miles-per-gallon. By either measure this overdrive-equipped 1951 Ford V-8 finished in the middle. (P)

Ford Motor Company executives gathered under portraits of Edsel and Henry Ford in the Administration Building conference room during 1952. Pictured from left to right are John R. Davis, Theodore O. Yntema, Benson Ford, John S. Bugas, Ernest R. Breech, Henry Ford II, Delmar S. Harder, Louis D. Crusoe, and William T. Gossett. Henry Ford II was president, Breech was executive vice president, and the others were operating and staff vice presidents. (P)

A crowning achievement of 1953, Ford's Golden Anniversary year, was the launch of the *William Clay Ford* on May 5. The 647-foot vessel was the third, and largest, ore-carrier commissioned by the company to haul raw materials to the Rouge. It was the Ford Fleet's first steam-turbine-powered ship. Later in the decade, Ford bought three additional ore ships and named them after former company executives. (D)

Top: Following the path of his father and older brothers, William Clay Ford drove the pace car for the 1953 Indianapolis 500-mile Race. The car itself, a specially-trimmed Ford Crestline Sunliner, was produced for customers in limited numbers as the industry's first pace-car commemorative. (N)

Middle: Benson Ford, vice president and general manager of Lincoln-Mercury Division, is pictured between 1953 editions of Mercury and Lincoln cars. Both had been modernized the previous year with new bodies. For 1952 Lincoln also introduced the company's first overhead-valve V-8 engine. (S)

Bottom: Lincoln participated in the 1952, 1953, and 1954 runnings of the Mexican Road Race with specially-prepared cars entered by private individuals, as well as by Lincoln-Mercury Division. The Lincoln's new 205-horsepower V-8 engine and state-of-the-art (by U.S. standards) chassis made it a formidable competitor and it won three "firsts" in its American sedan class. (W)

Although its North American cars were little changed for the Anniversary year, Ford did announce a completely redesigned line of trucks for 1953, and an all-new tractor, Model NAA. This is the half-ton F-100 6-Foot Pickup, a pioneer in the F-series that would become the world's best-selling vehicle. (N)

On its 50th birthday, June 16, 1953, Ford dedicated a new Research and Engineering Center, entered through this gateway in Dearborn. The R&E Center encompasses a majority of the company's scientific and technical activities, including the older Dearborn Proving Ground and 1923 Engineering Laboratories. (S)

This Vedette was the first postwar French Ford, based on designs for a never-built American small car resembling the 1949 Mercury. Production of the 2.2-liter V-8-powered line started in early 1949. After totally redesigning Vedette in 1954, Ford S.A.F. (the French company) was merged with SIMCA and later acquired by Chrysler. (N)

The "Whiz Kids," ex-Army Air Force statisticians hired by Ford in 1946, had moved into upper levels of management by the mid-1950s. Pictured in the front row of this 1947 photograph are Arjay Miller, Jack Reith, George Moore, James Wright, "Tex" Thornton, Wilbur Anderson, Charles Bosworth, Ben Mills, Edward Lundy, and Robert McNamara. (S)

The structural framework for Ford's new Central Office Building rose on "The American Road" in 1954 near the intersection of Michigan Avenue and Southfield Road in Dearborn. After it was occupied in 1956, employees called it "The Glass House." A later photo (p. 101) shows why. (R)

Long before the advent of Federal regulations, Ford conducted a series of crash tests prior to introducing a host of standard and optional safety features on its 1956 model cars. A pair of 1955 Ford sedans were sacrificed in this vehicle-to-vehicle collision. Today crash tests occur daily. (W)

Henry Ford II is pictured in 1955 behind his desk in the old Administration Building. When parts of the building's interior were remodeled shortly after World War II, this "modern" blond office décor replaced the Henry Ford-era dark mahogany paneling. The "modern" look remained until the structure was razed in 1997. (R)

This Continental Mark II was conceived as a reincarnation of the original Lincoln Continental, an image builder for the company. It was only available as a luxurious four-passenger coupe and, at $10,000, was the industry's highest-priced 1956 car. The car and Continental Division, headquartered at this exclusive plant, were discontinued after only 3,000 Mark IIs were built. (N)

Ford Motor Company became a publicly-held corporation in January 1956 and held its first stockholders' meeting in this tent at Dearborn Test Track later in the year. Ernest R. Breech had previously been named chairman of the board. Henry Ford II remained president. (R)

Body style innovation like this 1957 Ford Skyliner "retractable hardtop" was a key ingredient of Ford's competitive posture in the mid-1950s. Because they were built in relatively low numbers for only three model years, collectors eagerly seek "retractables" today. (S)

Although the two-place Thunderbird of 1955–1957 is most treasured by collectors, Ford created the four-place personal luxury car niche with this '58 model "Bird," and sales doubled. With a 113-inch wheelbase, unitized body and 300-horsepower V-8, it was built jointly with Lincoln in the new Wixom Plant. (W)

This C-Series variation, the company's first and most successful tilt-cab design, was new to the extensively changed 1957 Ford truck line. Like the Carling beer this one carried, C-Series is no longer marketed, but its 33-year life span made it a trucking legend. (W)

The Edsel car line unfortunately was introduced late in 1957 in a deep economic recession. It was intended to provide an additional medium-priced choice for upwardly-mobile Ford customers. Burdened with controversial styling, weak sales, and the heavy overhead of a start-up division, Edsel was discontinued on November 19, 1959. It became the classic symbol of failure. (N)

Edsel's Teletouch automatic transmission was electrically operated via steering wheel push buttons. (W)

On April 29, 1959 Ford produced its 50 millionth car, a Ford Galaxie sedan with a basic 292-cubic-inch V-8 rather than an upscale engine expected for a milestone. Young Henry joined visiting school children viewing the car at the Ford Rotunda. Pictures of earlier milestone vehicles are hanging in the background. (P)

The engineers involved in developing the 1960 Ford Falcon—the company's first North American compact car—gathered at the R&E Center for this photo. The Falcon, small by the American standards of the time, featured a 109-inch wheelbase and 144-cubic-inch six-cylinder engine, a design with lasting worldwide impact. (D)

When Ernest Breech retired in July 1960, Henry Ford II became chairman of the board. Robert McNamara replaced Ford as president on November 3. McNamara, previously head of the Car and Truck Group, resigned after less than two months to become Secretary of Defense. (N)

In 1958 Congress passed the Federal Automobile Information Disclosure Act, which required a label listing the suggested retail price of the car, optional equipment, and transportation charges. The label first appeared on 1959 models. This example was affixed to co-author James K. Wagner's first new car. (W)

Top: Ford Division's 1961 models were introduced at a novel press review staged in a typical American small town, Flora, Illinois, then the geographic population center of the U.S. One highlight of the event involved loaning every registered vehicle owner in town a new Ford for 30 days. Here a Ford Country Squire leads them in a downtown parade. (D)

Middle: Ford revolutionized the U.S. truck market with its van, pickup, and bus versions of the 1961 Econoline. It was based on Falcon running gear adapted to utility company needs and created a new market niche. While the pickup never caught on, the Econoline van and bus continue to lead their segments more than 40 years later. (W)

Bottom: Lincoln's completely redesigned 1961 Continental demonstrated that bulk was not necessary in American luxury automobiles. Cadillac had dominated the premium market since the early 1950s, but Lincoln rode this unadorned design to lasting competitive status over succeeding decades. (W)

An illuminated Ford Rotunda served as the backdrop for the company's new 1962 "intermediate-sized" cars: a Ford Fairlane (left) and a Mercury Meteor. These products created a new niche in the American auto market between compact and traditional large cars. The market forced GM to copy Ford's "product proliferation," which eroded its traditional "step-up" marketing system, eventually weakening GM's once-strong "medium-price" divisions. (W)

A fire resulting from a roof repair mishap destroyed Ford's landmark Rotunda on November 9, 1962. Built for the Chicago World's Fair, the gear-shaped visitor's reception center re-opened in Dearborn in 1936 but was closed to the public "for the duration" when it was used for wartime office space. It was remodeled in 1953 and a new façade was applied. The Rotunda served over 18 million visitors in its 26 years. (R)

Ford purchased the Philco Corporation in 1961 to help gain defense contracts. Beside its military electronics business, Philco assets featured a line of consumer goods, including radios, televisions, air conditioners, and kitchen appliances. The Philco assets became part of several organizations within Ford's Diversified Products Operations, but most were eventually sold and the company absorbed numerous former Philco employees. (W)

To commemorate Ford Motor Company's 1963 centennial of its founder's birth, grandson Henry Ford II sits at the wheel of a restored 1903 Ford in the Central Office Building lobby. The vehicle to his left is a 1963 Mercury, the company's 60 millionth vehicle. The graphic developed as a symbol of the anniversary hangs on the wall in the background. (R)

This *c.* 1962 aerial photo views Ford's Research and Engineering Center from the southwest. In the foreground along Rotunda Drive were buildings erected (from left) for Ford Product Engineering, Engineering Staff, and Lincoln-Mercury Product Engineering. Dearborn Inn and, beyond it, Dearborn Proving Ground (originally Ford Airport) are behind the center building. By then all car engineering had become centralized, and an expanding Truck Engineering activity occupied the former Lincoln-Mercury building. (P)

On April 17, 1964, Ford introduced another automotive genre at the New York World's Fair: the Mustang. The car became an instant success, indeed creating the subsequent "pony car" niche. The sporty-styled Mustang was based on a modified Falcon platform and shared functional components with the Fairlane, but incorporated unique body structures. It was initially available as a hardtop or convertible. (W)

Nine

WORLD AND GOVERNMENT CHALLENGES

1965–1982

In 1974, the three now-middle-aged Ford brothers posed symbolically in a replay of the famous photograph of them in front of their father's and grandfather's portraits taken some 21 years before (p. 81) at the time of Ford Motor Company's Golden Anniversary. Then it had seemed that Henry II would share power with his younger brothers. But it was not to be; there can be only one boss. Both remained company officers and directors. Benson became the company's ambassador to dealers, and William Clay bought the Detroit Lions football team for the focus of his attention. Henry ran the show as chairman of the board and chief executive officer, taking an active part in all company operations, although details were left to professional managers. Nevertheless, the rising corporate crisis in the 1970s was the issue of succession to his throne. (N)

Top: Both the full-sized "big" Ford and Mercury introduced major changes for 1965, based on a new perimeter-frame design. This is the near-luxury Ford LTD, which boasted of having a ride as quiet as the Rolls Royce. The Mercury won *Car Life* magazine's Car-of-the-Year Award with its many new features such as intermittent windshield wipers and rolling door locks, firsts at the time, which now are standard even on economy cars. (W)

Middle: Introduced in 1965, this Transit truck was the company's first truly multinational design and validated the Ford of Europe concept. To overcome nationalistic cultures, it was designed under U.S. direction jointly by Ford of Britain and Ford of Germany engineers, and manufactured in both countries. The Transit propelled Ford into a long-term leading position in European commercial vehicle sales. (W)

Bottom: Ford's original 1966 Bronco drew on the company's experience with a U.S. Army GP-replacement military vehicle contract and entered the embryonic four-wheel-drive sports-utility market in response to International Harvester's Scout. (W)

In less than two years, on March 2, 1966, Ford produced its one millionth Mustang, making the car one of the most successful in industry history. The achievement was marked by an ingenious arrangement of Mustangs outside the Ford Division headquarters for this aerial photo. Today 1965–1966 Mustangs remain among the most popular collector cars, unusual for a high-volume model. (N)

Ford Motor Company embarked on a new corporate identity program in the mid-1960s and established the one-time Ford script-in-oval hood ornament as its worldwide corporate symbol. The new sign, which replaced previous block lettering in use since the Forties, is shown in this 1967 photograph of the company's World Headquarters Building (formerly Central Office Building). (W)

The company was successful, but the mid-1960s were difficult times for Henry Ford II and his family. After the debuts of his daughters Anne and Charlotte, he divorced Anne, his wife of 23 years, and married Cristina Austin, an Italian divorcee. "The Deuce," as he was referred to irreverently by underlings, but never to his face, became something of an international figure. Here he is pictured in 1967 during Ford's successful forays to win the Le Mans races in France. (D)

During this unsettling period, Henry II also nursed doubts about the future management of the company. He recruited General Motors executive Semon Knudsen (center) to be president of Ford on February 6, 1968, elevating former "Whiz Kid" Arjay Miller from president to vice chairman. But the corporate "marriage" failed when Knudsen, who experienced difficulty fitting into a resistant Ford culture, was fired on September 3, 1969. (P)

Here are two examples of Ford's attempts to improve occupant safety. A "flower-pot" padded cylinder topped the 1967 steering column (left). The 1969 full-sized Ford had a swept-away instrument cluster (right) with the radio installed on the left side, out of the passenger impact zone in a frontal crash. This was the era when Federal Government regulations for safety and emissions were first imposed. (N)

This sleek "Techna" experimental car was one of many such vehicles built during the 1950s and 1960s and displayed to test public reaction. Co-author Michael W.R. Davis kneels beside the car in this photograph, taken in Washington, D.C. Among other features, the Techna had adjustable foot pedals, an advance only recently available on production cars. (D)

Knudsen's most visible legacy from his short tenure at Ford was the protruding front-end styling on two models, including this 1970 Thunderbird. Ford insiders called them "Knudsen noses." Such designs had been very successful for Knudsen at Pontiac a few years before, but were unwelcome in the new consumer-conscious climate. (N)

Lee Iacocca, a super-salesman armed with two engineering degrees, had an uncanny, seat-of-the-pants grasp of the auto industry. As "father of the Mustang" and other successful concepts, he rose from general manager of Ford Division in 1960 to president of Ford North American Automotive Operations in 1969. But Henry II had strong reservations about entrusting him to run the company. The two are shown here at a 1972 press conference. (N)

Equipped with a small four-cylinder engine imported from Ford of Britain, the 1971 Pinto was part of Ford's response to the foreign car surge headed by Volkswagen. Controlled laboratory testing of cars began to reduce proving-ground test-driving. Here a pre-programmed "shaker" in Ford's Reliability Laboratory simulates a rough road for a Pinto. (N)

Ford's continued response to the import invasion was again to bring in some of its European models, repeating a past practice. Lincoln-Mercury dealers sold the sporty German-built 1971 Capri, shown here being unloaded at a Detroit dock. (R)

This is an aerial photo of Ford's mammoth Michigan Casting Center, opened in 1972 at Flat Rock, Michigan, southwest of Detroit, near where a Ford village industry had operated in the 1930s. The company's plan was to replace obsolete and polluting Rouge foundries with advanced-technology casting capacity for large V-8 engines. Unfortunately, the technology proved to be flawed and the demand for large engines disappeared with the energy crisis of 1974. (N)

A grand celebration was held in 1971 to mark the 75th birthday of family matriarch Eleanor Clay (Mrs. Edsel B.) Ford. Her children, grandchildren, great-grandchildren, and spouses gathered for this rare family portrait. She died in 1976. Her influence saved the company in the difficult months after her husband's 1943 death, when she threatened her father-in-law, Henry, with selling her Ford stock if he did not turn over company reins to Henry II. (S)

Henry II's youngest child, Edsel Ford II, was the first fourth-generation Ford to join the company when he became a product-planning analyst after his graduation from Babson College. He is shown here with his fiancée, Cynthia Neskow, in 1973. They now have four children. The Edsel Ford II family keeps a low public profile. (R)

In the early 1970s, long before vans, minivans, and SUVs became popular, the family car was often a station wagon, and Ford (and Mercury) wagons ruled the road. This full-sized Ford wagon for 1973 featured a two-way tailgate—drop down or swing aside—and center-facing rear seats for youngsters that gave the vehicles a ten-person capacity. (N)

When the Arab-Israeli war of September 1973 broke out and the Arab embargo of oil shipments resulted, Ford was ready with a downsized 1974 Mustang II model, shown here with Lee Iacocca and an original 1965 Mustang in the background. The new Mustang, based on the economy Pinto, was puny and never caught on. Meanwhile, competitors continued building, and selling, real "muscle cars." (S)

Originally conceived for 1961 as a utility truck, the Econoline did not develop into a popular people-mover until this third generation model was introduced in 1975. Here a narrator extols such features as expanded capacity, "Captain's Chairs," and other comfort and convenience features shown in the cutaway body. Despite fuel prices that doubled after 1973, passenger vans were practical for those who needed to carry both people and cargo. (D/N)

Ford developed its first front-wheel-drive car, the Fiesta, for the European market in 1976, and imported it for sale by Ford dealers in 1978. Sales were limited because the Fiesta lacked the optional automatic transmission Americans wanted, and it was withdrawn from the U.S. market after three years while plans progressed for introduction of the American-built Escort for 1981. Modernized Fiesta versions are still popular in other parts of the world. (D)

Henry Ford II, always public-spirited, was deeply disturbed by the Detroit race riot of 1967. He became more involved in local civic affairs, investing in a new waterfront development, Renaissance Center, and worked together with Detroit's first African-American mayor, Coleman Young. Here they are shown together in 1976. (Ford grew the beard while recovering from an angina attack.) (R)

Most company marketing offices moved to Renaissance Center in the late-1970s. It's the backdrop for this photo of the new 1977 Lincoln Versailles model. Ironically, 20-some years later, Ford's arch-competitor General Motors bought Renaissance Center (popularly called ("RenCen") from investors at a bargain price, and turned it into its own new world headquarters after Ford offices departed. (W)

The stylish Continental first envisaged by Edsel B. Ford in 1939 underwent several generations of change through the years. When the top-of-the-line 1977 Continental Mark V came out (front), it was posed with its predecessors, a 1941 (upper left), a 1956 Mark II (left center), a 1969 Mark III (upper right), and a Mark IV (introduced for 1972; a '75 or '76 shown). (N)

Disturbed by personal problems including an angina attack and failing second marriage, Henry II appeared indecisive in some corporate matters. But in April 1977 he dealt with uncertainties over the car market and a "palace revolution" by creating an "Office of Chief Executive" in which Ford President Iacocca (left) had to share power with new Vice Chairman Philip Caldwell (right). Henry II fired Iacocca in July 1978, and the latter went on to a notable second career at Chrysler. (N)

The 1978 Ford Fairmont, shown here in initial production at the Kansas City plant, and its Mercury partner, the Zephyr, were designed on an all-new "Fox" platform as a replacement for the Falcon chassis used for Maverick, Comet, Granada, and Monarch. The basic Fox design continues today, a quarter of a century later, as an underpinning of the 2003 Ford Mustang. (N)

Another long-lasting and highly profitable platform for Ford passenger cars has been the "Panther" design, introduced in 1978 for the down-sized 1979 Ford LTD and Mercury Marquis. This Country Squire wagon was top of the Ford line. The 2003 Lincoln Town Car, Ford Crown Victoria, and Mercury Grand Marquis are built on an updated Panther platform. (W)

This 1979 Mustang was Ford's 150 millionth vehicle, a number representing worldwide production. Vice Chairman William Clay Ford, President Philip Caldwell, and Chairman and Chief Executive Officer Henry Ford II posed with the recently built car on December 14, 1978. Henry II resigned as chief executive officer October 1, 1979. Six months later, he turned over the Chairman post to Caldwell, and Donald Petersen was elected president. For the first time in 77 years, no family member served as an operating executive of the company. (S)

Ford obtained a 25 percent interest in Toyo Kogyo of Japan (later renamed Mazda) late in 1979. Toyo Kogyo had been building Ford-branded compact Courier pickup trucks, such as this 1979 model, for Ford sale in North America and other markets. Mazda has played an increasing role in Ford's worldwide business ever since. (N)

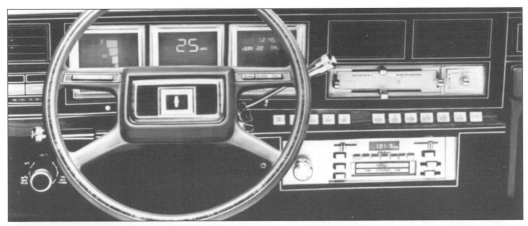

Top: Ford became a leader in automotive electronic technology with this electronic instrument panel on 1980 Lincoln and Continental models. Much of the technology evolved from Ford's investments in Philco and Ford Aerospace, although those activities had been largely phased out by then. (N)

Middle: The 1980 Lincoln Continental was a foot shorter and 800 pounds lighter than its predecessors and the first all-new senior car for the company in a decade. Mounted on the "Panther" platform, it continued little changed but highly successful for another ten years. Its Town Car designation began with 1981 models. (N)

Ford introduced its first U.S. front-wheel-drive cars with the 1981 Ford Escort and Mercury Lynx. Henry II's daughters, Anne (left) and Charlotte, produced a book, *How to Love the Car in your Life,* whose cover featured them with the new cars. A European Escort went on sale at the same time and, while generally similar, shared only its powertrain with the U.S. cars. Ford still promoted the Escort as a "World Car." (W)

Ford's Michigan Casting Center got the contract to cast the blocks for the new 1.6-liter four-cylinder Escort engine, shown here being processed. The contract wasn't enough to fill the plant's production capacity designed for 7.5-liter engines a decade earlier. Also burdened with inefficient use of energy, the plant closed in 1982. (R)

By the early 1980s, Ford felt the competitive pressures worldwide from low-cost, high-quality Japanese vehicle producers. Another of Ford's multinational efforts was this medium-duty Cargo truck, designed in Europe for production there and in Brazil, and eventually also manufactured in the U.S. (W)

114

Ten

THE NEW GENERATIONS

1982–2003

The third and fourth generations of the Ford Dynasty posed here during Ford Motor Company's 90th Anniversary celebration in 1993. Standing in front of the Greenfield Village replica of the company's Mack Avenue plant are Edsel B. Ford II, William Clay Ford, and William Clay Ford Jr. At the time Edsel II was president of Ford Motor Credit Company while Bill Ford Jr., as he prefers to be called, was general manager of Climate Control Operations. Bill had joined the company as a product-planning analyst after graduating from Princeton in 1979. During the decade that followed this photo, the fourth generation would face some of the greatest challenges in the company's almost 100-year history. Bill was chosen by the family in 1998 to run the company. Edsel turned to both public service and other business enterprises, while remaining a director and consultant. Bill became chairman of the board on January 1, 1999 and chief executive officer on October 30, 2001. (N)

These were the members of Ford's Office of the Chief Executive in 1982: Will M. Caldwell, Donald E. Petersen, Philip Caldwell and William Clay Ford. They were pictured with two new car models: a European Granada (left), and a downsized Lincoln Continental. (W)

This Georgian mansion on Lake Shore Drive in Grosse Pointe Shores, Michigan, was home to the Henry Ford II family starting in 1956. The house was razed in 1983. Ford had lived there with his first two wives but moved to a smaller residence off the lake after marrying Kathleen DuRoss. (S)

Henry Ford II is shown with his third wife, Kathleen, at a social event in the mid-1980s. Ford, who had retired from official management of the company by this time, was still active behind the scenes until his death in Detroit on September 29, 1987. (N)

Top: When sale of imported compact pickup trucks reached a critical mass in the late 1970s, Ford Truck Operations initiated an appropriate response. Introduced in early 1982 as a 1983 model, the Ford Ranger shown above soon overtook its Chevrolet S-10 competitor to lead the market segment. (W)

Middle: After stumbling badly with stodgy-looking 1980–1982 Ford Thunderbird and Mercury Cougar personal luxury cars, the company responded vigorously in 1983. This new aerodynamic "jelly-bean" styled Thunderbird established Ford as industry design leader. President Donald Petersen is widely credited for inspiring this new direction. (W)

Bottom: Ford of Europe launched the Sierra, a compact upscale sedan with sprightly performance. It was fitted with a Brazilian-built, turbocharged, fuel-injected engine in 1985 and brought to North America where Lincoln-Mercury dealers sold it as the Merkur XR4Ti. *Merkur* is German for mercury. (W)

Top: The 1986 Ford Taurus followed Thunderbird's lead and broke the conservative mid-size automobile styling mold with its aerodynamic theme. Taurus and its Mercury Sable cousin were also the company's first intermediates to incorporate front-wheel drive and an all-new 3-liter V-6 engine. (W)

Middle: Mercury Sable and Ford Taurus were available in station wagon as well as sedan body types. Sable also featured an industry styling innovation: the light bar. It integrated flush-mounted headlamps with an illuminated center section in lieu of a grille. (W)

Bottom: Attending the Board of Directors product orientation for 1987 models in September 1986 at Michigan Proving Ground were President Harold Poling, Henry Ford II, and Chairman Donald E. Petersen. (N)

After Chrysler Corporation established the front-wheel-drive minivan market niche by developing an abandoned Ford design concept, Ford Motor Company responded with this rear-drive Aerostar. (W)

Foreshadowing the end of Ford's Fleet, the *Henry Ford II* passed under the raised Dix Avenue Bridge as it left the Rouge plant c. 1985. The last of Ford's original ore-carriers, she was sold for scrap in 1989. (D)

Ford merged its earlier purchase of Sperry New Holland with Ford's Tractor and Diesel Engine Operations to form Ford New Holland, Inc. on January 1, 1987. Pictured are the integrated product lines: Ford tractors and New Holland equipment. Ford New Holland was sold to Fiat in 1991. (W)

119

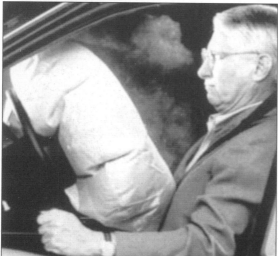

Gathered around contemporary Ford Motor Company cars in 1990 were members of the Office of Chief Executive: Philip Benton, Stanley Seneker, Harold Poling, and Allan Gilmour. Significantly, no Ford family member was then among these veteran executives in the OCE. (W)

Lincoln Continental adopted standard airbag supplemental restraint systems for 1990 models. The driver-side system was mounted in the steering wheel pad and the passenger-side unit behind the instrument panel. A Ford Public Affairs executive braved a test airbag deployment for this photograph. (N)

Following ten years as purely a Ford design, the all-new Escort for 1991 became an adaptation of an existing Mazda vehicle. Under a new strategy, Ford assigned small car engineering to its Japanese affiliate. (W)

Top: Ford redefined the sport utility vehicle (SUV) market with this Ranger-based 1991 Explorer. It took the genre to a higher level of space, luxury, and convenience, thereby gaining the market leadership the Explorer still held a dozen years later. A shorter, two-door version concurrently replaced the existing Bronco II. (W)

Middle: The company turned to another Japanese manufacturer, Nissan, for assistance in providing a distinctive minivan for Mercury dealers. A joint venture resulted in this 1993 Mercury Villager, which was based on Nissan's Quest design. Ford assembled both vehicles at its Avon Lake, Ohio, plant. (W)

Bottom: Scottish-born Alexander J. Trotman, pictured with an array of 1994 models, succeeded Harold Poling as chairman in 1993. He was the company's first CEO to be knighted by the British monarchy, but rarely used his title in America. His massive, and controversial, corporate restructuring plan, "Ford 2000," was announced in 1994. (W)

Henry Ford III, great-great grandson of company founder Henry Ford, helped celebrate the 100th anniversary of the 1896 Quadricycle at Greenfield Village with his father, Edsel Ford II. This was also Henry III's 15th birthday, and after leaving the tiller of the Quadricycle replica, he obtained his driver's learning permit at the Dearborn Police Department. (S)

Early in 1997, a Ford Motor Company landmark was razed, the 3000 Schaefer Road former Administration Building near the Rouge complex. It served as corporate headquarters between 1928 and 1956. It then became home to Lincoln-Mercury Division and later was headquarters for Ford Parts and Service Division. (P)

Opposite, Top: Although it had just introduced totally redesigned models, including this AeroMax highway tractor, Ford sold its heavy truck business to Daimler-Benz-owned Freightliner in 1997. Since the redesigns were the first in 27 years, the rationale and timing for divesting this world-class product still has Ford Truck followers puzzled. (W)

Opposite, Middle Left: Ford introduced the 1998 Lincoln Navigator, an ultra-luxurious SUV and Lincoln's first "truck" in modern history. The new offering pioneered a highly-profitable new market niche for Ford Motor Company. (W)

Opposite, Middle Right: Ford also announced a limited-production electric-powered edition of its popular Ranger compact pickup for 1998. Most buyers have been public utilities and government agencies. (W)

Opposite, Bottom: This Lincoln LS, a new smaller model that shared the Jaguar S-Type platform and illustrated the company's globalization strategy (Ford purchased Jaguar in 1990), attracted the most attention among Lincoln's 2000 models. (W)

Top: This 2000 Jaguar S-Type was the first "Jag" co-designed with an American model, potentially extremely profitable in the European luxury sedan market. In contrast, the 1964 Jaguar S (rear) was typical of British touring sedans—semi-hand-built and costly. (F)

Middle: Early in 1999, Ford announced it would purchase the passenger car business of Sweden's AB Volvo. As a key member of Ford's new Premier Automotive Group (PAG), Volvo provided Ford an additional entrée to the worldwide market for high-technology European cars. This 2002 S80 is the top-of-the-line Volvo. (F)

Bottom: Ford had purchased British manufacturers Aston Martin Lagonda Limited and AC Cars Limited in late 1987. AML provided Ford with a stable of ultra-expensive sports cars, the pinnacle of which was this limited-production $150,000-plus Aston Martin Vanquish V-12. (F)

The capstone to Ford Motor Company's global acquisition spree came with purchase of the Land Rover business from BMW Group on June 30, 2000. This line brought to PAG a prestigious family of sport utility vehicles, enabling effective competition with BMW, Mercedes, and Lexus SUVs. This is the Land Rover Range Rover for 2003. (F)

The centennial of the Ford Dynasty's participation in auto racing was celebrated at Greenfield Village in September 2001. To highlight the event, Edsel Ford II drove this replica of his great-grandfather's race car in a reenactment of the latter's duel with the Winton Bullet. (F)

Elena Ford, Henry Ford II's granddaughter and daughter of Charlotte Ford and Greek shipping magnate Stavros Niarkos, was first of the fifth generation of Fords to join the company. Ms. Ford, brand manager for Mercury vehicle lines, is pictured here with a 2002 Mountaineer SUV. (F)

125

Top: Ford followed its discontinuation of the personal luxury Thunderbird in 1997 with a promise to revive the two-place original. After an extended period of publicity, the new Thunderbird, styled much like the 1950s car, emerged in 2002. It has been a sell-out success. (W)

Middle: The 2003 Ford Crown Victoria appropriately represents the 100th Anniversary Ford car since it is the direct descendent of the original Model A. As *the* Ford car, it was once the company's bread-and-butter product, but now its customer base is primarily law enforcement agencies and taxi fleets. (W)

Bottom: During the 2003 calendar year, the Mercury car line will reach "retirement age" (65), but is enjoying an active life as the car of choice for senior citizens in the United States. This 300-horsepower high-performance Marauder model has been added to the line to broaden the brand's appeal. (W)

The 2003 Lincoln Town Car received the model's third revamping since adopting the sturdy rear-drive "Panther" platform in 1980. The Town Car is one of America's most popular full-sized luxury cars, whose large, if aging, group of owners may not always appreciate its technical advances. (W)

A smiling Bill Ford Jr. points the way as Ford President Jacques Nasser rides into the distance on the company's Think! electric bicycle at the 2000 North American International Auto Show. After serving in the position less than three years, Nasser resigned on October 29, 2001, amidst a sea of corporate red ink and internal turmoil. (F)

Nick Scheele succeeded Nasser as company president. A British subject, he is credited with making Jaguar a profitable enterprise and resurrecting Ford of Europe. Here he shares a platform with Bill Ford Jr. to answer questions about company progress. (F)

Co-authors Michael W.R. Davis (left) and James K. Wagner are pictured with their 2002 Ford Focus automobiles in front of Ford World Headquarters. Focus, the latest and most successful of the company's "World Cars" went on sale in Europe in autumn 1998. Its North American debut was for the 2000 model year. Replacing the famous Ford script-in-oval on the building facade is the latest corporate signature, which displays the company's full name. (D)